Counting the Chiperoni

Also by Adèle Ogiér Jones and published by Ginninderra Press

Poetry

Afghanistan – waiting for the bus
From the Edge of the Pacific
Beyond the Blackbird Field
Sense of Place (Pocket Poets)
Blantyre Leaves (Pocket Poets)

Fiction

Desert Diya

Adèle Ogiér Jones

Counting the Chiperoni

Counting the Chiperoni
ISBN 978 1 76041 741 3
Copyright © Adèle Ogiér Jones 2019
Cover photo by the author, from Zomba Plateau

First published 2019 by
GINNINDERRA PRESS
PO Box 3461 Port Adelaide 5015
www.ginninderrapress.com.au

Contents

Chiperoni and cloud	9
Landlocked	11
Counting the Chiperoni	12
From the ocean	13
Old home of stone	14
Chiperoni	15
Calling fog	16
Floating on clouds	17
Tea plantation	18
Raising the cloud	19
Bush and plantation	21
From the khonde	23
Border highway	24
Wilderness story	25
Bush remedies	26
Songs on jungle leaves	27
Jungle overhead	28
Storm	29
Soche Hill	30
Overture	31
Breaking ground	32
Dreaming	33
Counterpoint	34
Impala	35
On winter's eve	36
Concert	37
Intruder	38
Silent gecko	39
Poem in an address book	40

Mbira	41
Shadow	42
Watching sun disappear	43
Arranged marriage	44
Reading tea leaves	45
African tulips	46
Zomba Plateau	47
Morning laughter	48
And their people	**49**
The woman on the hill	51
Sonnet on wilderness	52
On loss	53
Ash Wednesday	54
Livingstone	55
Letter to Mrs Livingstone	57
Packaging	58
Homeward ferry	59
Rastas	60
Ilala	61
Kwa Haraba	62
Moneyman	64
Limbe Leaf	65
Green gold	66
After harvest	67
May Day fantasy	68
From the factory	69
At the station	70
Limbe train	72
Tumaini	73
Blantyre library	75
His response	76

Sonnet for the ferryman	77
From a land called Z	78
Land Cruisers	80
Charcoal carriers	81
First day of May	82
Last night's conversation	83
On reading Nadine Gordimer	84
Gordimer	85
Tambala	86
On Partridge Road	87
Capital	88
On the road to William Falls	89
112 days	90
Intersection	91
Transiting through Addis	92

Chiperoni and cloud

Landlocked

Where is Blantyre and the Mpingwe of whom you speak?

At the bottom south-east tip where it's held
in the cupped hand of Mozambique,
Tanzania its cap at the northern end.

And where are these others from the letters you send?

Zambia borders east, jutting quietly into the land
and in the centre – a lake shared by another,
with islands held by both, no longer disputed
one or the other, Mozambique or Malawi.

Brothers now, both claiming their own,
invisible lines known clearly to each
though fishermen refuse to notice.

Counting the Chiperoni

It could be the Chiperoni settling
over the hills and valleys far below,
we'll not know if it is here to stay
until another three hours have passed,
lifting by ten
then just cloud passing
up here on Mpingwe
at the end of the Partridge Road turn.

Coming from the sea straight as the birds fly
from Mozambique
across villages speaking
the same tongues
colonisers' languages foisted
on families intermarrying, separated
by the road from Lilongwe in one direction
Zimbabwe in the other.

Chiperoni its introduction
in villages along the way
where storekeepers sell what is forbidden
on one side
legal on the other
their smiles and the secrets the same,
counting the days
for Chiperoni to lift.

From the ocean

Three days of fog and cloud
over our mountain
three days from Mozambique's coast
and India's ocean,
a triple package they predict
more accurate than the mantelpiece clock
for they've known it
forever.

This lasts for one of them
then glorious blue skies and sunshine
until heavy rains lash at Thyolo
over tea plantations
while I sit as dry as parchment
in the drawing room at the planter's lodge
seeing only old photos on history's walls,
forgetting workers outside.

Old home of stone

Creeping cautiously, silently
unannounced,
there for the thinking of it
like you, before the morning
pronounced
between the *khonde* and the old home of stone
on the hill, reflecting another
now rock denuded
unadorned
like the pure fog of thought
entering dreams in the dark
your presence too
visit unannounced there
in the shadows, without sound
until woken, realising the dream
a message from afar
but no ringing of bells
or tapping on window panes
for you are fine
like the mist
which silently lifts and disappears
into the morning sun
so quickly that sadness fills its place
on this Mpingwe hill.

Chiperoni

High from the *khonde*
greeting invisible guests
Chiperoni calls,
mystery floating
uninvited
graciously
wrapping its white mantle
around bare grey hills,
silent whiteness
greeting dawn
with the offering of fog's calm.

On other days
sun seeps through
as cloud over the valley
blows sweeping sounds
away in the wind
from the seed broom on the path,
bustling breezes through trees
birds soft still,
nearly eight as the gate opens
and workers greet each other
in muted voices.

Calling fog

Fog releasing night
mares giving birth in the field
before morning sun

around the *khonde*
wrapping Chiperoni arms
softer than feathers

as dawn fog lingers
promising calm for the day
contradicting none.

Floating on clouds

Maybe this is what heaven is like
living in a cloud moving silently
with life all around,
papery leaves rustling in the old tree
hanging over the stone house,

little birds chirping – one two three
modzi wiri tatu
in the bushes and gardens
above the woman's grotto,

children's voices
ringing from somewhere in the valley below
Bangwe wakening,
gardeners walking round like angels
tending pot plants thriving
in this gossamer Chiperoni.

Tea plantation

Tea plantations wrap the estate owner's house
in mantles of green
throughout the year
and through the fog
when clouds settle
green oozes as primeval slime
might have done when the great sea
covered the land.

Mist clouds the green quilt round the house
closeting the outhouses
and planned garden below
with its fantasies transported
transplanting a nobility for less noble exploits
hiding all from workers trudging
through red quagmire
mud up to their knees.

Raising the cloud

Silently cloud passing through
as early morning fog
over the dry table and cushions
lone sentries on the *khonde*,
droplets of night's tears
soaking the damp foam
covered in fake African design,

then slowly lifting
in a straight line on the horizon,
a crow travelling along with it
marking the edge
like white screens lifting slowly
fog drifting upwards
towards clouds waiting formation.

Bush and plantation

From the khonde

(Playing Father and Son)

Looking down to where you are
Where I've been, isn't easy
Thinking now you're far away
Far beyond the edge of time.
    Can you hear me when I call
    Through the clouds on the *khonde*
    Looking out across the plains
    Towards savannah heartlands dry.
Looking out from the *khonde*
Where we met so very briefly
You, that day long ago
When the year was very young.
    You had to go away beyond
    My feeling and our dreaming
    To the place outside the mountains
    Far enough to lose our dreams.
Looking across the barren mountains
Stripped of all old vegetation
To the clouds of unknowing
Out to where you laughed at night.
    You said it all once long before
    That we could never to the land belong
    It is more than just the language
    More than stories lost in time.
And shadows of lost rainbows
Far beyond the recollections
Waiting still up on the *khonde*
on the edge of memory's hill.

Border highway

Highway from the capital branches
where a signpost shows Mozambique
and the traveller knows further still stands Mugabe's place.

Straight on, the road leads to Blantyre
named for a town across oceans away
so different, one wonders the sense of it.

On one bank Malawi lies slumbering,
across the tarmac a neighbouring land
speaking Portuguese for the claimants.

English on the other as logical or not
where today Airtel signs settle comfortably
on both, no matter the language of market.

Scattered along the road, locals know what lies there
charcoal illegal on the left, tomatoes better on the right
where neighbours cross for better health prospects.

Where cousins gave kin refuge in conflict,
their words the same language and meaning
safe haven, known customs their right.

Now governments turn blind eyes where a road
shows no borders, travelling between
countries once one, buried in yesteryear's dust.

Wilderness story

Wandering, wondering on wilderness
encroaching suburbs where past bush stood,
lone forest creatures one with the homeless
diverted traffic flows where once was wood,

fresh lawns replacing wild undergrowth
irregularity's art disappears
leaving stark coastline where duplexes boast
vacancy, to let, advertised all year

attracting new adventurers seeking
relief from the concrete surrounding them,
sea stretching past horizon releasing
forgotten memories of an ancient time

before waking to find old wildlife gone
And with them their people's stories and song.

Bush remedies

Wilderness has gone without trace
where tea plantations exact and precise
replace the jungle and bush boasting their remedies
secret recipes, birds, and creatures traversing
conversing in other tongues shared in passing
on flights to cooler climes
and water
forgotten in the taste of tea.

Black and green, and in pride of place
silver tips, queen of the plantation
and beyond it in the planter's house,
replanted in the style and times of people
newly settled, far from where the sun shone rarely
skies thick and heavy like veils
protecting women's *zenana* quarters
from the world.

And here the fog
lingering still across the hills
unchanging
the blanket of rainbow greens
a velvet shadow offering false security
in photographs posted,
bush fading
forgotten.

Songs on jungle leaves

Here coffee beans and tea leaves have replaced
a jungle landscape where people hunted,
collecting other seeds and fruits which graced
their blankets, blessed by game on which they fed

until the planters and their kindred came
surveying with their eager eyes, new lands
on which to grow their crops with little shame
all claimed in the name of a crown's demands,

hillside's field repainting jungle's rainbow
where songs have lost melodic nesting birds
fleeing patchwork nets and spinning arrows
with new plantation rules replacing words

once sung across the early morning sky,
their sol-fa hymns sung loud in sole reply.

Jungle overhead

Flash of red from crimson poinsettia in the green
above the palm tree planted by the rock
left standing long before
the colonisers and monied claimed
this hill
forgotten now in cash-gate time
with fertilised, soaked, diverted aid,
coming long before grand houses
on other hills on the way to the airport,
where still tiny birds flit
twittering between hued trees
in a lost earth's Eden.

Species strange
midst flame trees still boasting pride of place,
shadows on rocks capturing grey silhouettes
of tiny yellow birds
and grander reds and blues if they dare come this morning,
bright sunlight mocking early clouds
settled in valleys until they fade and melt
on this early Easter feast
reminders of days through other gates
other stories, where shocked frowns and heads shaking
dismissed bleak stories of embezzlement
called otherwise here in Mpingwe bush.

Storm

Wild is the beating of my heart against the pane
glassed in without the world seeing that it's there
cold framed around the landscape far beyond
today's and yesterday's fury and madness
of the wind across the plain
wild, desolate, begging for a drop
receiving nought
even with the thunder
rolling overhead
and inside thoughts
where lightning flashes
without relief
of rain.

Soche Hill

Someone has walked this way before,
a stone with golden word *stronger*
left for the walker or the next happening upon this place
at the top of the hill above the iron bridge
where the wooden virgin stands
child in her arms
and on her back the suffering man
the child will become.

The one who carved from wood
this virgin gazing down, loving
calm for the child about to spring from her arms,
carved and formed this sculptured piece
with love
African lips, closed in the soft smile
nose flared, breathing in, contented.

Anyone happening on this grove
hidden in rocks looking over Mount Soche
might think it ancient
boulders thrown up in a cataclysm
long past
perhaps an ancient spirit place
where lizards now dart in and out
midst patches of warm sunlight
safe in the shadows thrown by these rocks.

Overture

Just before seven you come
boisterous, beautiful, insistent
in case I never knew of your presence,
a hint of a melody, then swelling
your proposal to another
somewhere in the distance,

as if meant for me
warm to meet the still-cool morning
and I answer your call
somewhere near, in the foliage above
near enough but little to show
for the wonder of your seduction.

Dull grey, overlooked
save for the full-throated demands
enticing the other to answer
and I tread, aware presence
crushing and crunching stones
will disturb your song's persistence.

Hidden, to your bowered space
I turn, and you move
circling to lower branches beyond the stone wall,
as above, from the tallest tree
comes your lover's call, answering briefly
your pleading now silent.

Breaking ground

Pockmarked and pimpled
hill at the end of the range
dismally groaning
weighed down by houses creeping ever higher,
face of a teen as old as the land
where loads of concrete
crush the spine
sadly torn
broken after forest harvesting
till nothing remains.

Villages in bush where brilliant birds once sang
overtaken by settlements
roads through
paved with promises
for new electioneering
holding firm for their vehicles but none beyond
where before, footsteps up bush tracks
found enough
and plenty more
for their magic of life.

Dreaming

Yesterday
orange butterflies flittered
and dove through the bush,
their white cousins
settled further down
where the poinsettia is in full bloom.

Today
a couple of grand black fairies
as big as bantam birds
resting on power lines far below
make one deep sweep
and disappear from the same place.

Watching
thinking of that other bush,
our own far away
and the colours living there,
then flashes disappointment
recalling her grandeur beyond words.

Counterpoint

Crows raucous across the valley
hens somewhere below
or late-night roosters,
flocks of sparrows twittering near
dull thudding electrified villages as midday nears
and ringing from the minaret within
undercurrent overlooked, ignored
even there refusing to be put down.

Thinking on again and watching butterflies
too soft to join the throng
sole bee interrupts
then a bush fly
and a bellbird
single, solitary, in the distance.

One might be alone in the bush
on the hill above the town
from where the train horns out
in counterpoint to traffic and factory
industry producing its own sound
the raucous noise
for those departing
even in the dead of night.

Impala

Still, listening with head tilted, seeking reassurance that the dull sound on the horizon beyond the twittering birds where sun sinks, confirms that the rumbling is from church bells in the distance, somewhere out along the road to a smaller town once deemed capital, for they found it cool, just as impala might this evening,

No twitch or shudder to give its place away to hunter or beast greater and hungrier than itself, secure in the dullest colours of the forest evening, sensing the chaperoning fog creeping around the corner, up the path, invisible still until it descends, escape impossible.

One slow movement, and it halts. A tree creaks eerily as a bird mimics in reply, another songster reassuring, nearby. It treads one step, hesitates, nostrils quivering, seeking the invisible intruder set to disturb the balance of this place.

A gentle murmur across the sunset hairs down its back, white speckled snow freckles where it never snows, shivering in reply to the old tree's frog tone, hinting that evening will come with its own protection.

For impala, comforted clan is within reach, this moment between seasons at dusk's puberty, promises and threats show in the trembling whiskers of its sundown hide.

On winter's eve

There is something about a soft May afternoon
before it is time for sunset
still warm enough though it will not last long
green all around
refusing to drop
refusing to bend.

And I think of golden poplars
along other roads far away
planted in a place where they too do not belong
adapting
singing in the autumn
which suits them.

Gone the frangipanis
sole sign that it's almost winter
red flame trumpets boast
light here in May the same
silent, caressing
with a sun about to disrobe before us all.

Concert

All in the time it takes
an hour hand to do full circuit
to match your circuitous concert
this morning,
an orchestra pit
without tickets or bookings
anticipation
always rewarded:

Ten reep oo, ten reep oo, ten reep oo ten reep!

painting your love call
composing it
unable to see you
or describe beyond your signalling

Trip ee trip, trip ee trip, trip ee trip –

a change, disappointed
the questioning satisfaction gone,
then
a trip a trip oo – so softly
is it you?
then silence,
lost cadenza.

Intruder

Mosquito-netting tent shrouds the unwilling sleeper
tormented by the humming
which persistent tinnitus buzzing cannot drown.
torturer, why waitest thou until the dark
envelops me?
why hide until I am almost at that point
of no return,
delicious sleep.

then diving, spinning nearer
as if to drown me with thy scream.
if only this delightful resting place,
this tent
which even the richest sheikh would claim
could keep thee out,
protect me
from thy boastful siren.

Silent gecko

High on the wall
beyond the picture frame
silently slithering, scampering
still until soft movement and noise
or the light from the evening lamp
disturbs the sunset sleeping.

Sudden the spring
hidden, blending again
as one more decoration
in the house designed by another long before
remembering the planter's wife
before it became the pilot's place.

Nothing changed
gecko remains in place
more at home than any painting, candle or vase
of dried flowers trying to make it like a place
with some history they will call home
sole rest for none beyond itself.

Poem in an address book

And in the cold bitter night
breaking brittle wire netting
rusting across the window pane
no longer able to withstand
lazy mosquitoes
too dull to search for blood in this empty house
where the long, sad howl
of the night-train sounds
on the way to nowhere
promising sugar and tobacco
for the season is now.

Mbira

I knew you were watching as I sang my song
Ave ave to the forest
Observing with an ear turned in the wrong direction
Just as I do with a deafness inflicted too soon,
As if to catch the whistle on the wind
Spirits of ancestors from the bush
Or another animal forced to move
In search of vegetation, theirs like yours
Destroyed by ceaseless schemes for charcoal,
Ancient growth near the cloud line aflame.

I sensed your scrutiny, observing Mbira
Disturbed from your midday winter warmth sleep
Another migration
Along with the others seeking better life
And seclusion
Far from the savannah,
Out on that far branch over the valley
Transit to the next port of call
Where they won't catch you, at least today
Out of sight.

Shadow

Imagine a hard, cream candle
burning low
casting a shadow caused by eyes no longer sharp
some strange condition creeping slowly.

Imagine this candle
not bees wax, painted with black bees
huge bees of the forest thick on the hill behind
where purple bushes grow wild
too wild for cultivation
no salvia, lavender, or rosemary
too thin to be irises, too wild to be cousins to the grand azalea
along the path to the top.

No violets there, nothing so delicate or secret
in a bush and land thick with butterflies
and signs of animals never sighted,
dried-out turds hinting to hidden
souls visiting or visited by climbers
ignoring the sign declaring
forbidden, progress at your own risk
on the mountain from where no one returns
on Mlange.

Watching sun disappear

No words left today beyond the faint pink clouds out there
with their purple-grey underbellies,
flat, painted, waiting to dry
irregular dimensions like the feeling
looking at flat posts others post
of themselves for Facebook friends,
telling a hundred stories without words
or messages
thin, hair tied back, grimace
like a line-up mug shot.

What is it you're saying
as the clouds stretch out and flatten
greyer in spirits on this afternoon's
early sunset
melting before dusk over the hills beyond Mpingwe,
wasted, with no tears left
to bolster them,
nothing African about them,
all life and colour gone
on the eve of winter's month.

Arranged marriage

Arranged yet unexpected
some satisfaction, even love
and the thought of leaving, sadness and regret
arranged, with its own delights
birds singing, clouds lifting
flowers coming and blooming
and through it all, spathodea
the orange-red tree aflame
trumpeting
falling once it opens
this African tulip tree.

Reading tea leaves

Strange wild storms predicted on last night's news
forgotten as the morning sun reveals
far mountains peppered with pale sugar dew
like icing on a wedding cake conceals
sweet longing.
        Now reading leaves once foreign
        deemed reliable, as warnings of heat
        escort moths to maize crops where they crunch long
        devouring while nature struggles to meet
need as
dried-out land and hailstoned crops face
wild confrontation never seen before,
and withered kitchen garden leaves replace
green once mirrored in tea estates next door,
        where storytellers claim they never dreamt
        earth's fury could shatter environment.

African tulips

Along the road leading into the place on the hill
out of bounds for all save those passing through from the
village below
fences repulsing
blocking those who built the place
deterring all save those who care for the land and its produce
and the birds who settle regardless
singing in the tulip trees
beside the pathway which leaves them in peace.

Bold in the air reaching far into the clouds
beyond easy picking except where blooms
fall in mid-morning's warmth, fine vases
futile for brash flames without stems
held in dull shaded rooms,
decoration where sun cannot reach
stragglers demanding attention
shouting from the *khonde* where they've blown.

Zomba Plateau

Zenith
    Over
        Morning
            Breaking
                Across

Plains
    Lying
        Ancient,
            Trodden
                Expectantly
                    Again
                        Unaware

Plains
    Listening
        Anxiously
            Towards
                Eagles
                    Attacking
                      Unsuspecting

Plains
    Lying
        Anguished
            Threatened
                Exploited,
                    Axes
                          Uncontrolled.

Morning laughter

Shadows from mountains
where laughing waterfalls lurk
dulling early glee,

mountain ridges shout
exploding morning sunburst
strokes their nubile breasts,

laughter on the way
tumbling stream dodging rocks
youthful skittishness

with Zomba waiting
water's falling gifts above
the tranquil morning.

And their people

The woman on the hill

She didn't call today or even show herself
that woman on the hill
beyond the future
at cedars in the valley below
where they told me she would be
dressed in flowing robes of morning
gossamer and evening twilight dust
if she thought to come to meet again
those dreaming of tomorrow
a fresh glimpse for tired eyes
and limbs and spirits jaded
by affairs of state, empty coffers and pockets
intent on the day and its needs,
dreaming of someone like
herself
someone to remind them of myths and fairy tales
and promises
beyond their reckonings and boredom
beyond the corruptions and greed
all around
reported in newspapers,
those who never mentioned
the woman on the hill
beyond the blue grass and cedars.

Sonnet on wilderness

Alone they trudge with little more than hope
across a land where others long before
had searched for signs of timid antelope
at peace while grazing on the valley floor,

but rains have ceased and wildlife travel far
in search of pastures wild across the plains
in turn the tribes have lost their guiding star
so drift to towns where contract work remains

and finding there a wildness never known
manufactured substances transforming
their minds and lives with little left to show
beside meagre sums they're paid each morning

here where the wild has turned to desolate
lost wilderness ignored by governments.

On loss

How do peoples wake each day to face land
they know was stolen from their parents
and theirs before them
can there be forgiveness, acceptance, reconciling?

Done stealthily
without realisation and understanding
land no longer performing as it did
crying in desecration, degradation,

while others talk finally of environment
decrying new agreements to lease
and mine the land no longer virgin
with new rape and upheaval

as earth cries silently.

Ash Wednesday

The muezzin calls this early morning's Wednesday
at the foot of the hill where the road winds up,
with a bell in the distance from the cathedral
out on the road to Zomba
long protected by the woman
who says nothing but apparently sees all,
while there's silence
outside the Limbe leaf factory

for it's too early for harvest and sorting
for packing and carriage
to the railway station down the road
where the old steamer still goes
to god knows where
competing with crops at the ports
across the hills in the neighbouring land,
too early yet for golden brown harvest
still green in the distance
beside sugar plantations in rain,

too early for their slashing and burning
leaving ash
and little else
for what's left of villages
depleted
once reaping season descends.

Livingstone

There is a letter hidden in a secluded corner of the museum outside Blantyre, a museum rarely visited, dusty and grey, lights weak in load-shedding, never deemed important enough to illuminate empty spaces and sparse glass cabinets, though in one lies the letter.

Six pages in script legible. David Livingstone it is signed, as dull as its storage place, telling more of the activity of that day – implements and containers, who had seen what and whom else, asking questions of those back home, thanking them for their kind correspondence, and outlining needs.

And to this day the Scottish Blantyre continues with links and affinity, with the town named after it in a warmer land, known less now for missionaries and explorers, and more for new real estate developers, for industry which never took off has been overtaken.

And young ones head out south or to the land of Livingstone's folk in search of work, a brain drain like so many more, and those who can go, do. For what is asked of them seems too great, where what counts is who is known to whom, and favours still to be repaid.

So Livingstone's letter gathers dust and in time, will crumble in the heat or gather mould and brown spots from humid days which the dull light globe in the cabinet case does little to address.

David Livingstone, signed and dated, purple ink, and script handsomely strong, in this failing economy where they debate still if they can work with democracy, their first old man saying not, relying on his own authority.

Letter to Mrs Livingstone

They laid her to rest near the great baobab tree
at a place which became utter wilderness,
war ravaged and matted with jungle grasses
trodden only by beasts of the forest.
He had written that no face was as dear
or as kind to him as her sunburnt one
and she wrote back
with letters long crossing seas
that since his leaving
on one more expedition
she had never passed a dreamless night
or knew an easy day.

And he said of her, broken hearted when she was gone
that a right straightforward woman
with no crooked way she was
decisive, with energy when required
but still he went
leaving her grieving
out of place in a Victorian England,
then in the bush with hidden spirits to boost
failing energy, repeated steps
journeying where gentility would not
across Kalahari sands to the man
whose name overshadowed her.

Packaging

The wrapper claims this tea was not packed
by children
alerting unsuspecting minds, innocent, acquiescent
customers and travellers who have read it elsewhere,
carpets and footballs and electronics
which tiny, thin fingers can do cheaply
what machines do not
and adults want not.

Still others work
collecting plastic from landfill
stacks reaching high into steaming skies
where smoking stench escapes
noxious, poisoning stink beyond belief and knowing
on the edge of cities and places not far from towns
where tiny bodies and brains
are too fast destroyed.

Pain in their putrid cradles
unseen by customers' incredulity,
invisible stories
left on vacant shelves
of supermarkets
as wild in their own ways
as those children
pack unheeded.

Homeward ferry

As boys they would catch the train from Limbe
to somewhere much closer to the lake
and then three days sailing to the next point
frightening these land locked lads
who saw no shores
for such is the size of this sea.

He said the boats were better then,
much safer than now in state of disrepair
and there was a famous boatman
the best sailor of them all.

And they tried for his watch,
his boat and his steerage
but maybe he has gone
four decades since that time.

The train is no longer used
by boys and other travellers now,
vehicles faster, though no safer
no time for the sauntering creature
they called the caterpillar,
no time for the boat home.

Why take three days with nothing to do
on school holidays and Christmas
nothing to keep young minds occupied
except singing and storytelling?

Why go this way for three days
when one by road means home
to the gossip and family meddling and arguing
after the first night and its tales are over?

Rastas

Rastas none too popular
when they sing their smoky songs
kind to kindred and kinsman of other clans who look to them
look to any who might show some concern to needs
of a friend of two, taking them as they are
even though not one of them.

There is one with a woven rainbow hat
hanging to his shoulders holding locks kept firm,
another land's sufi or saint perhaps
befriending wild creatures, singing to birds
as brothers, crooning gently for his sisters
who understand pebbles for marriage.

Quiet enough around their village
until some outburst hits the media, misbehaviour
then it's headlines in Malawi Times as police
describe some other public sin, in their eyes
outsiders who live to revive the light
to realise the dreams of their eyes.

Ilala

Nadine Gordimer said that she had seen women do it:

rolling *ilala* fibres
up and down and across
naked thighs,
palms wrapped, worn hands
as hard as the earth where they sit
languidly
languishing in hope
of customers.

Ilala
sign aptly chosen
for an overnight
sojourn
where travellers and adventurers
dream still
of a storybook
lost Africa.

Kwa Haraba

Splashed bright, paint across skies
and wooden tables where reggae music plays
early in the morning
at the artists' place
hidden from mainstream regular events
artisans and poets on Wednesday evening
known by the few
smoking a rare cigarette.

Artists beyond dreams
and expectations
beyond grand places
with Italian names
and intentions
as if tastes with European labels
la caverna, café grazie
prove better.

Here, bloody marvellous,
haraba sundowner,
and even monkey business
taste different from cappuccino, affogato
and double espresso
though these they have
as well
at Kwa Haraba,

the joint
where writers with laptops
compose in seclusion
away from project meetings at Sunbird
cold, brittle and dry
with few expectations
beyond cash and per diems,
while artistry murmurs on at Kwa Haraba.

Moneyman

Why do they call it 'moneyman' I ask
you say
that is where the old drive-in theatre used to be
we had such, I say
and we talk of it – that time before videos, DVDs and television
why the name 'moneyman' I ask
you say
that's where the young men went to drink
and before that
where they played soccer, and then there was the sports field
now a football ground
and we talk of the Wanderers and the Big Bullets
and of northerners and southerners fighting
after football games
and losses and successes
and why those from the north are so different from the south,
and culture and schooling
and of preparing young girls to service
old men
and of houses for maidens, their brothers somewhere else
too old to live together
or old enough to wander through the night
initiation never mentioned
puberty suggested
but dark stories and many more
which makes me wonder still about
money
and men.

Limbe Leaf

Away out of town on the Limbe side
long before the Chiradzulu turnoff,
Mpingwe mountain where the tea sheds
stand, below the hill overlooking the tide
of people wandering in when endorsed
or waiting in silence for word of work
at the factory all call Limbe Leaf,
less judgement than calling it tobacco.

Here few smoke this stuff
prices prohibitive
sold only in places with foreign names,
here seasonal gratitude their concern
for harvesting then sorting for grading
before buyers turn up to auctions,
sweet odours wafting
their only concern.

Green gold

Few complain of tobacco plantations, it is more despair that Mozambique has overtaken them, though others still boast the country does well with their sales, customers still coming for auctions, last season's prices high.

It is only with digging that a deeper truth surfaces, that family lands were sold, used now for tobacco, where they give up their own crops to follow this path, whole families involved in the project, with sales to middlemen offering meagre reward though they know they are far down the ladder.

And with the seasonal proceeds locked into banks, and moneylenders waiting nearby for repayment of loans, comes yet one more advance for the season, for last year's scatterings and perhaps the one before, with interest incurred.

Then to the market to purchase what once they grew, more cost than their labour, and children out of school caught in cycles of production, unsold leaf in the over-packed market, lower prices, and dreams up in smoke.

After harvest

Orange butterflies
skating across shining leaves
like ice skaters
impervious to the gaze of onlookers.

Crows calling, regal like midnight cousins
dressed in white shirts and dinner jackets,
like waiters behind tables
attentive to slight movements
anticipating desires, demanding attention
grand in their own way.

All in their own worlds
above the life with the music below,
reggae suiting crowds milling
resigned outside tobacco works down along the road.

The canvas of rusted rooves
patterned and fitting, regal in their way
yet overshadowed by flour mill towers beyond,
each with its own story
as people gather on workers' day
now the harvesting season has come.

With promises of work to last the year
morning crowds silent, expecting to be chosen
on the broken road outside Partridge Road sheds
just as their fathers did, and their fathers before them.

May Day fantasy

On the way to Limbe Leaf
at the end of harvest season
tobacco auctions ring loud
while workers resigned
grateful for the gathering
and the sorting and packing to come
work on
through this day dedicated to them
ignoring international fantasy
knowing only that today
is another
for overtime.

From the factory

A siren blasts from the rusted factory
below the tobacco-coloured iron roof,
sorting and packing inside
with minutes in between,
whistles and horns from a train
pulling in, shunting out of Limbe station
now past its glory days
here where workers move in and out
starting overtime
down time and down payments
on this public May Day
holiday.

At the station

One might just as well be invisible for all the notice given by those around the station and over near the shunting sheds, unseen in the bustle of workers with their deadlines to meet, loading, reloading, dragging sacks, as heavy and dull as the labourers themselves, dead on their feet, there since before daybreak, broken before their time, no more than boys many of them. It is hard to tell through the coal dust and white powder they say is from flour sacks destined for bakeries down the road.

One more day the same as the rest at this time when wagons rich with coal and wood and contraband depart for the south or head off north, leaving villages empty in this transit season, gold tinkling at tobacco auctions, lighting the eyes of traders, unseen by men and women on the factory floor, and on platforms soon crowded, transiting lives overtaken by flying trucks and over-packed minibuses.

On the station, there is no longer a smart master in uniform of navy blue with its braid denoting rank, master capped to indicate importance, his status enhanced with a shining whistle, silver mined nearby, and his right to distinguish between first and second-class passengers, and others fitting no classification.

Now, only a warm jacket in winter, refuse from the second-hand clothes at the market, sent over from Europe, meant as donation but costing nevertheless, or belonging to his father or father before him, always a he, where the women stay back in the sheds with the packing and sorting, labelling and disguising records, sweeping droppings from sacks and from mice hiding to devour what is left overnight.

For an outsider, a dismal place, but for those who see beyond the grime and dust which they never dream might be a hazard, a place where they might say with pride, *I work on the railways*, just as fathers have done. Casual work in season which leaves an imprint, joking and retribution built into stories they tell back home after it's done at the end of the busiest time of the year.

Limbe train

It takes a day to reach Blantyre
too long and uncomfortable
they tell me
puzzled that anyone would think of train as an option,

though overcrowded mini buses
carrying contraband
from Mozambique and Mugabe's place,
with passengers beyond the limit
swerve off roads
to private tracks
if road traffic authorities are seen before them,
police stops no problems.

Quick meetings behind vans
hands shake, empty palms filled by shrewd drivers
and after these necessities, throttles roar
as life goes on.

Railways, though, are another story
carrying sugar
and now, at harvest time
with auctions in full swing,
tobacco leaf carried noisily
invisibly,
for smoking futures
where crops once stood.

Tumaini

In Swahili
there is some hope remaining
in a word refugees use
with its promise of a chance
where there are no borders to speak of
only tribal clans claiming their wandering
for hunting, for gathering
where the wild over-planting had demanded
new boundaries and borders
guarding jewels earth has yet to offer
the unsuspecting foragers
who tread the old land.

Others watch migrating herds
in the wet season
where they too swelter in hope of discovering
what will keep them beyond tomorrow,
celebrating and storing far beyond beauty
decoration swaying with the steps on savannah treks,
sturdy nether regions for the grand marches
which are to follow in the dry
when the game is too rare and mean
at empty waterholes
where only the bravest will venture
seeking to survive.

Tumaini, co-opted for their language of flight
the wandering to calm, word has it
peaceful for people accepting,
accommodating brothers' tongues and meaning,
sisters' beauty and care,
Tumaini, adopted to explain it all
so no shock remains, no despair
replacing hope, as others go further north
to face seas until turned back
deemed unsuitable to claim refuge
where their word is not known,
they will whisper it, understanding.

Blantyre library

He tells me what he remembers happily from school
going to an old public library,
the *Tintin* books with Captain Haddock,
then James Hardy Chase,
and onto the *Merchant of Venice*,
its Shylock in particular he recalls.

And *Lord of the Flies*
(book I detested)
and he tells me the point and the lesson of characters
like life, he says
conflict and struggle, and false leadership,
he's seen it all.

Then finally
(as if justice has won out)
two African novels,
he names them well for *Things Fall Apart*
and we know for sure
there's *The River Between*.

His response

And the other delight came after I gave him two shirts
to replace that torn
when he carried furniture for the office set-up.

The minute the buckle was snapped tight in the car
he took a Phil Collins cassette,
inserted it in a contraption hidden by grime,
played loudly
non-stop
for the rest of the day
and the next two days
until the weekend.

I forget what it was called
something about love
so I waited to see what would happen next.

Sonnet for the ferryman

The ferryman was once well-known round here
by children going home along the lake
he'd be there through the year in weather clear
his job they knew, like breath he'd not forsake

lost children kept at schools throughout the term
hoping for life better than their elders
false dreams of merit through the things they'd learn
relieving old mothers' burdened shoulders,

their laughter never daunted by the man
whose frown was grim when faced with looming storm
and once all boarded then the song began
with others joining in the glad refrain,

while songs and stories over years relayed
could never tell how helmsman learnt his trade.

From a land called Z

And you told me near the sunbird
where the others' laughter drifted
of your father and your years
of bleakest darkness, torment
after they had taken him and his life
before your eyes,
the father waiting by the crossing
to meet you after school,
how you heard a shot
then saw a crowd
gathered by the body
underfoot.

And you told me of your father
in opposition to the land grab
saying this is not the way,
that man of law belonging not
to those who ruled
with fists and claims of iron
determined their way was right
claims of government
beyond the law
no better than land usurpers they replaced.

With breath, they robbed your youth
replacing with nightmares
the dreams of equal place and harmony
of which he spoke,
with lurid sounds and images of fear
a suicidal future left instead
as you fled the place,
the only way to face tomorrow
forgetting stories which were your own,
adopting anew, his name for life.

Land Cruisers

In smart white Land Cruisers it is easy to listen to claims
that travelling in local buses is handing
your life away,
overcrowded and packed like pilchards
in cans sealed tight from outside,
prisoners on each-other's laps
for unexpected desires,
speeding, no attention to rules
for those with new found status, not fitting neatly
these workers and drivers and government officers
in white Land Cruisers,
where cost and wayside stops
beyond new highways
are no problem.

Through Land Cruisers' tinted windows
it is easy to look down
on the road
to those sitting on sacks too heavy to carry,
on empty crates at the end of the market day
near mud patches which once marked tracks
as landing places and loading bays
on the way up the hillside beyond,
before the rainy season
where villagers roam still
along paths where white Land Rovers
dare not crawl.

Charcoal carriers

As ants crawling up hills
men and boys dragging bicycles laden with grey charcoal
sugar bags spilling out onto tarmac the same colour
broken and melting in hot sun,
middle men so police leave them alone on side stops
along the way before Bangwe road check,
authorities part of it
slicing and chopping, sawing and bull-dozing forests
for charcoal and cash.

Hills left bare like eggs aged with mildew fungus
denuded
offensive
like breasts of young girls
barely in menses
men ogling, lips dripping
saliva for virgins,
forest slowly turning to rock again,

Winds and the frosts and clouds of corruption
with other names
wear away at the rock
hiding jewels for collection,
riches for cooking and warmth
for morning peoples
herders and bushmen,
this day's power cuts load-shedding for new amenities
stripping bare, their dance without exaltation.

First day of May

May Day but no maypole here
where trees are cut down as soon as they have budded
like young virgins unfrocked
ravaged
destroyed
bleeding blue guns like menses' first blood,
deflowered, the rape
rights which have come with new customs and governing
rights claimed though all was in common
if not taken by them, then others
officers, uniforms
bargaining without fear of criminality
no thought of future beyond the year,
this season's pocket and purse.

For charcoal burning
without desire beyond this midday,
morning's broken promises,
acts at dawn or late at night
when saws and trucks and axes
desecrate a fast-changing landscape,
forest disappearing
leaving scars and grizzled whiskers
where once songs sang
earth left flowing down hillsides, calling creatures lost
outside game-parks where tourists and romantics go
to see wild animals, reimported
on backs of trucks
across the bare land.

Last night's conversation

Last night I watched Nadine Gordimer on *Hard Talk*
honest talk, clear and pure
about inverted racism
her desire for a new people
with love between lovers
new children and a new population.

But she talked of corruption's naiveté
of how they had not thought it through
her own party, her own beloved
worse than the rest
a corruption entrenched,
ground into their bones.

On reading Nadine Gordimer

Reading nadine gordimer
page sixty
description
without verbs
without completion
no objects
subjects
and left wondering
how to do it
consistently
with power
to set in memory
images
sufficient.

Gordimer

New approach
unhindered by conventions of sentence
and construction
in the hotel room
where, without mother
there were no books
no flowers
not at all like home
her father's house
the construction she saw
standing in relation to the hotel
as does a child's cupboard
full of treasures
to its parents' domain,
light through burglar bars
and elsewhere
sunset light dappling the walls
of her father's prison cell.

Tambala

They will not go to school he claims
tambala is to blame
girls and boys live separate
in houses far away from family
now of a certain age
so they roam around at night he says
dancing all the hours
too tired for school
too overcome with what has gone on
through the darkness
when grandparents sleep with forgotten dreams.

On Partridge Road

Out on the road where the fog lifts
forgetting the time
between morning and darkness
with night barely gone,
casual, seasonal workers gather outside Limbe Leaf
along Partridge Road.

I know it for cool, fresh morning dampness
keeps one in bed
warmth tempting
regretting the cold floor outside
while sessional staff
small men dressed for church or some special occasion
gather quietly along Partridge Road
and the roads at the T-junction
waiting for work,
the selection call and invitation
as if dress makes a difference when it comes to tobacco sorting
but word has that it does.

Capital

Cash-gate
now maize-gate
and grand houses
secluded
hidden
behind gates and walls
guarded, protected
out of sight
and beyond touch
from the roads where we walk
wondering
why it has come to this.

On the road to William Falls

Past quiet men selling stones or wishing to,
standing forlornly
leaning against an old tree whispering it has seen it all before,
young men shy, dispirited by slow custom
watch walkers rare on the red track on the way to the waterfall,
passing women bent by burdens of wood
destined for the fire market
in distant Zomba below,
stooping youngsters, too small to carry
loads of fresh branches
fallen they assure
for cutting trees planted in a forest of pine generation
forbidden, though ebony appears in curio stalls
along the road near Ku Chawe inn.

Silent waiting,
covered by night tarpaulins
safe from marauding hands
searching and reselling, their attempts
another waste of time,
incessant bargaining for a better price
to capture masquerading blackened objects
no longer used for pianoforte,
rare things long forgotten here
except in the tourist trade
and old colonisers' guest houses
abodes of that other era, best forgotten
in this forest, on the road winding up to the waterfall
gurgling down to the dam it has made for itself.

112 days

Trumped again by the man on the screen
saying it has never been as good as this
his one hundred overshadowing mine
with twelve more,
looking to a different phase
restringing the violin
adjusting the tune and the tone,
different drumbeat to match
a new dance
along the same path
over the valley
beneath the *khonde*,
then on up the road to the red poinsettia
beaming down from the green jungle
below the ochre rock on the hill
and another flash of crimson beyond it.

Intersection

Local women waiting for sales
observe dawdling youths
in token imitation of foreign mates
revving the dust beneath their wheels
skylarking
near the top of the hill
where they cut through the walled gardens
short cut
from the villages below,
on the hill which tells two stories.

Transiting through Addis

Stranded birds in flight
hover precariously
waiting for sunrise
where
desert caravans
with songs of people meeting
at noble crossroads
halt
stranded with stories
at crossroads of history
between cloud and stone.

www.ingramcontent.com/pod-product-compliance
Lightning Source LLC
Chambersburg PA
CBHW062139100526
44589CB00014B/1625